Sometimes I Have to Tell You, "No"

Amanda Sorg

AuthorHouse™
1663 Liberty Drive
Bloomington, IN 47403
www.authorhouse.com
Phone: 833-262-8899

Because of the dynamic nature of the Internet, any web addresses or links contained in this book may have changed since publication and may no longer be valid. The views expressed in this work are solely those of the author and do not necessarily reflect the views of the publisher, and the publisher hereby disclaims any responsibility for them.

Any people depicted in stock imagery provided by Getty Images are models, and such images are being used for illustrative purposes only.
Certain stock imagery © Getty Images.

This book is printed on acid-free paper.

ISBN: 978-1-6655-1991-5 (sc)
ISBN: 978-1-6655-1992-2 (e)

Print information available on the last page.

Published by AuthorHouse 03/12/2021

authorHOUSE®

For Clinton and Harrison.
And I'll always love you.

_____

Sometimes I have to tell you, "No."

Sometimes I have to make you mad

My job isn't to make you angry,

It's to make you a good man.

Sometimes I have to tell you, "No."

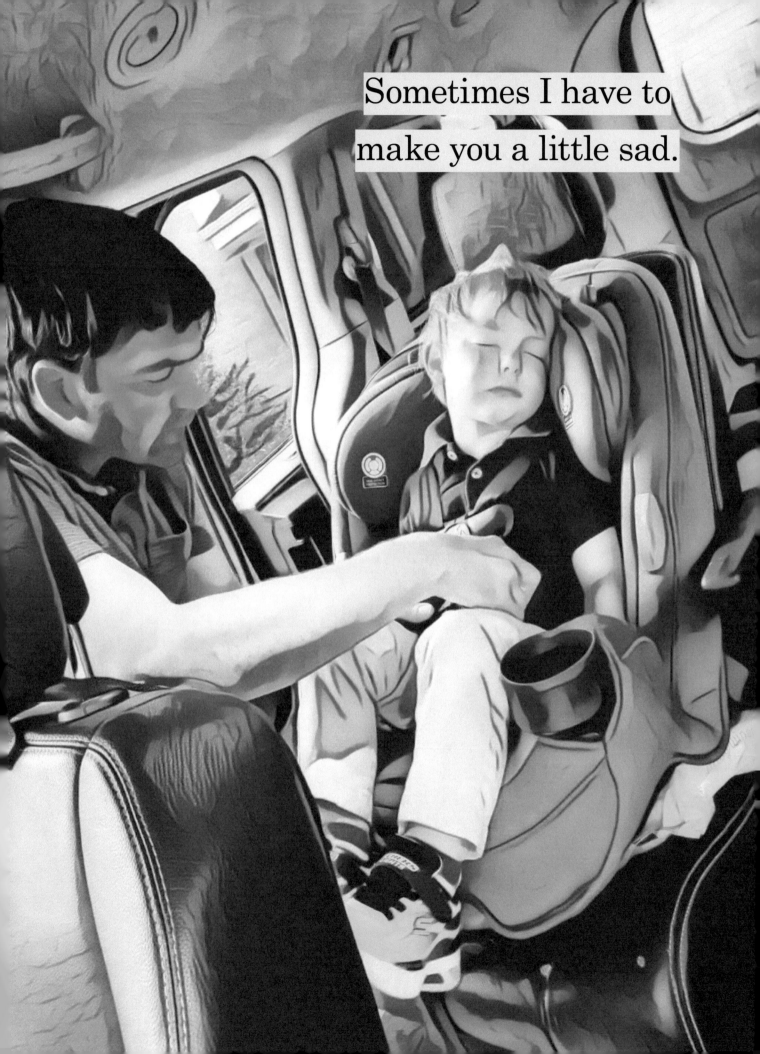

Sometimes I have to make you a little sad.

You won't grow up
to know what you really have.

Sometimes I have to tell you, "No."

Sometimes the answer cannot be, "Yes."

It doesn't always feel like it,

But "no" is sometimes best.

Even though we may not agree

Two things are always true

You'll always have me

And I'll always love you.

Printed in the United States
by Baker & Taylor Publisher Services